Living Discipleship

David Jenkins

NATIONAL CHRISTIAN EDUCATION COUNCIL

Other worship resources published by NCEC

Celebrating Series . . .
A series of six books for all-age festival services:
Celebrating Christmas Books 1 & 2
Celebrating Lent & Easter Books 1 & 2
Celebrating Harvest
Celebrating Special Sundays

Anthologies of material for private reflection and public worship
A Word in Season
Liturgy of Life
Flowing Streams
Prayers for the Church Community

Cover design: Julian Smith
Cover photo: Sonia Halliday

Published by:
National Christian Education Council
Robert Denholm House
Nutfield
Redhill, RH1 4HW

British Library Cataloguing-in-Publication Data:
A catalogue record for this book is available
from the British Library.

ISBN 0-7197-0827-3

First published 1994
© 1994 David Jenkins

Typeset by Avonset, Midsomer Norton, nr. Bath
Printed in Great Britain by
Clifford Frost Ltd., Wimbledon, London

CONTENTS

FOREWORD TO THE SERIES

This is the fifth in a series of six books which offer services of worship for all ages in the church. The details of the other five can be found on the back cover of the book.

The authors write from a wide experience of leading all-age worship and the *Living Worship series* . . . springs from that experience.

In the celebration of Christian worship every age-group has something to contribute. The experiences of each member of the congregation, regardless of age, can be used, and should be valued. The ability and willingness of children to enter into a wide range of worship experiences should not be under-estimated. Adults should be encouraged to accept the gifts which children bring to worship.

There is no 'audience' in all age worship. The children are not performing for the adults; neither are they passive spectators to adult worship. These services provide the means by which the whole church family can engage in its most important responsibility and joy: the worship of God through Jesus Christ.

These books will serve churches best when a group of people, representative of all ages in the church meet to plan the worship, and are prepared to give time and thought to the preparation. Those who use them should feel free to adapt them to the needs of the local church community. In any one church they may well emerge on a Sunday morning looking quite different from the details given on the printed pages that follow.

Unless the flow of the service requires it, no place is given for either the Lord's Prayer, the offertory, or announcements. These should be included according to local practice.

Series Editor: Donald Hilton

4

PREFACE

Amidst the tumult and tension of a crazy world, Jesus calls people of all nationalities and ages to follow him into danger and delight. The call to discipleship rings down the centuries, persistent, compelling, urgent. The writers of the Gospels heard it; the apostles heard it as did Jews, Gentiles, slaves, free, women and men. All responded through transformed lives, filled with energy and love.

These four services provide opportunities to reflect on the joy and challenge of discipleship. They may be used most profitably during the period of Lent, yet need not be confined to this period of the year.

Follow Me explores the challenge, joy and surprise of discipleship. *Many Times Forgiven* proclaims the good news that discipleship is not a journey for perfect people, but a response to God's forgiving love. This service is particularly suitable for Ash Wednesday or the First Sunday in Lent.

The third service is entitled *Living Water*. It is a service of renewal, recalling the meaning of our Baptism and celebrating the resource of 'Living Water' which is a sign of Jesus' presence. The final service centres upon Jerusalem as a goal of Jesus' journey. *City of Palms* asks, 'what is the goal of discipleship?' It pictures the scene in that city and explores the hopes and dreams of the participants.

David Jenkins

FOLLOW ME

Introduction

Discipleship is an invitation to a journey. Jesus calls people of all ages and backgrounds to share the risk of travelling to an unknown destination. It is easy to slip into the danger of believing that Jesus' journey was all mapped out for him. However, we should remember that the Gospels were written long after the events they describe. During his lifetime Jesus had to accept each event as it occurred, not knowing what was going to happen next, and thus had to make decisions that were incredibly difficult. It led him from Galilee to Jerusalem, and eventually to his death.

Following Jesus today involves many decisions and poses many questions. This service is based upon some of the questions we might ask about the challenge of discipleship then and now.

Preparation

Arrange a table and chairs at the front of the church for the kitchen scene. Travel magazines should cover the table. Seven people are needed to become 'question marks'. Attach a cardboard question mark to a headband and add a 'dot' on their noses! They may either wear sashes with the relevant question on: (Where? When? Whose? Who? What? How much? Why?) or carry placards so that the words can be seen by the congregation.

Rehearse the drama. It will be greatly enhanced if the participants do not carry scripts. Adapt the suggested ideas to include local place names. The Pied Piper should ideally play his/her own instrument. If this is not possible, it could be mimed to notes played on a reed stop of the organ or on a keyboard. Choose a reader with a clear strong voice who will stand off-centre to read the succession of short readings.

ORDER OF SERVICE

Call to worship   *Use five voices. Photocopy, duplicate, or use an overhead projector so that the congregation can share the call to worship. Alternatively, the words given to the 'congregation' can be spoken by a small group.*

VOICE 1	And God called out to his created universe:
CONGREGATION	Come alive with my word of power.
	Follow me into my glorious future.
VOICE 1	And God saw all that he had created, and it was good!
VOICE 2	And God called out to man and woman and child:
CONGREGATION	'Come alive with my word of power,
	Follow me into my glorious future'!
VOICE 2	And God saw all that he had created, and it was good!
VOICE 3	And God called out to Abraham and Sarah, to Moses and Miriam, to Jeremiah and Isaiah, to Ruth and Naomi:
CONGREGATION	Come alive with my word of power.
	Follow me into my glorious future.
VOICE 3	And God saw all that he had created, and it was good!
VOICE 4	And God called out to Jesus of Nazareth:
CONGREGATION	Come alive with my word of power.
	Follow me into my glorious future.
VOICE 4	And God said: 'This is my precious son, listen to him'.
VOICE 5	And Jesus said:
CONGREGATION	Come alive with my word of power.
	Follow me into my glorious future.
VOICE 5	'Dance then wherever you may be,
	I am the Lord of the dance', said he
	And I'll lead you all wherever you may be
	'And I'll lead you all in the dance', said he.

Hymn   'I danced in the morning'

Prayer

Living God,
long, long ago you called your creation to come alive,
and ever since that time
You have invited people to follow you on an exciting journey.
Today we come to thank you
for the way you have touched our lives,
calling us to follow without fear.
Grant that we may be strengthened and encouraged
by our worship this day.
Renew within each of us
the conviction that you are our friend and leader:
that you will never expect us
to face things you have not experienced yourself;
that you wish our journey to be enriching and enlivening.
Remind us of the personal way you relate to each of us,
so that you become for us,
not a rule book to obey
but a person to know.

We ask this through Jesus Christ our Lord. Amen

Reading   Mark 1.16-20

Leader

That all sounds so easy doesn't it? Did Simon and Andrew and James and John know what they were getting into? Of course they didn't. They had no idea. It sounds as though a strange man just comes out of the blue and asks them to follow him. Even if they already knew Jesus, which is quite possible, it all seems remarkably strange to us! We would have asked hundreds of questions before setting out. It's just like planning our holidays . . .

Drama

In an everyday kitchen, Mum, Dad, and two children (Tim and Suzannah) are sitting around the kitchen table on which is a pile of holiday brochures. Use the following conversation or write one to suit your situation. Keep it light and humorous. No matter how you do it, seven questions need to emerge: **Where?**; **When?**; **Whose?**; **Who?**; **What?**; **How much?**; **Why?** *These questions need to be displayed to the congregation as they are raised in the conversation. See the Preparation section for suggestions on how to do this.*

9

TIM	OK let's get this over quickly. I've got to go out tonight!
SUZANNAH	You're not going out with Lisa Hadlee. She's the size of a double decker . . .
TIM *(Interrupting)*	She is not!
SUZANNAH	She is . . .
MUM *(Interrupting)*	Now, now, now, if you go on like that, we'll put you on separate desert islands for your holidays!
DAD	Ice-flows would be better. Let's get started. The question is: Where are we going for our holidays?

*The question **'Where?'** is shown to the congregation*

MUM	Well, I'm for going back to Scotland. We could pop in to see Aunt Maud on the way. How about a cottage on Skye?
TIM	Scotland? It's frozen there, and rainy. I camped on Mull once and won first prize.
SUZANNAH	I bet you didn't What for?
TIM	Swimming under water, and that was inside the tent!
DAD	Here's an interesting brochure. How about a longboat on the French canals.
TIM	Oh, oui, oui, oui. No, that's too slow for me, but at least we're getting warmer.
MUM	We could take a package holiday, Spain, the Canaries, Sicily.
SUZANNAH	Now you're talking.
DAD	Well, when are we intending to go?

*The question **'When?'** is shown to the congregation*

MUM	We're limited to the first two weeks in August because we need to be at home when the examination results come out.
TIM	My friend Greg had a great time in Majorca. He said the night life was fantastic.
DAD	The Thomas's went to the Greek Islands and said it was quiet. It depends whose is the recommendation!
TIM	He's been watching Shirley Valentine!

10

> *The question 'Whose?' is shown to the congregation*

SUZANNAH   Can we bring our friends, if they pay?
DAD   Well, that does raise the question of who is going
           with us.

> *The question 'Who?' is shown to the congregation*

MUM   If we go on a package holiday you will be bound
           to meet new friends when you arrive.
DAD   It seems to me that there's a far more important
           question we need to answer first: What do we
           want to do? What's on the programme? Do we
           want to walk, to sit on the beach, to sleep. . .

> *The question 'What?' is shown to the congregation*

SUZANNAH   Well, I know that I want a good tan.
TIM   Yes, I know where too!
MUM   Tim!
TIM   OK, OK. Well, How much have we got to spend?
           Shouldn't we ask that as well?

> *The question 'How much?' is shown to the congregation*

DAD   I don't think we'll ever agree on what we want, but
           I do reckon we could afford a basic package
           holiday for two weeks. Let's take this one here.
           There's a beach for Suzannah, walks for Mum and
           I, and an evening disco for Tim.
SUZANNAH   Where is it? Cleethorpes?
DAD   No, it's in Portugal. We can fly direct from
           Manchester.
TIM   And if that's not available, what about the Greek
           Islands?
MUM   So that's settled, but there's one question we never
           asked: Why have a holiday?
SUZANNAH
and TIM   Oh, Mum!

> *The question 'Why?' is shown to the congregation*

Hymn   'O Jesus, I have promised'

11

Leader
So now we have our seven questions. They are the same questions we ask at many times in our lives.

Where shall we go?   **When** shall we set off?
Whose is the recommendation?   **Who** is going with us?
What's on the programme?   **How much** will it cost?
      Why are we going?

They are the seven questions we need to ask about what it means to set off on a journey to follow Jesus.

Hymn   'Will you come and follow me'

As the hymn concludes a Pied Piper figure enters playing the tune-line on a flute or recorder. The Pied Piper invites a few people to follow her/him as they move round the congregation. They finish at the front of the church and the followers sit at the Pied Piper's feet.

Leader
Jesus said, 'Will you come and follow me.' But we have all sorts of questions: The first is: 'Where shall we go?'
While this is being said, the piper and followers move towards the person representing question mark 'Where?' and calls him/her to join the line, moves around the church, and then returns to the front.
Where shall we go? Listen to this.

Reader   *(From off centre)*
     John 14.5-7

Prayer   *(Led by 'Where?')*
    Jesus, you are the direction we shall go.
    Help us to read about you, think about you, dream about you,
    so that you become for us the Way, the Truth and the Life.
                Amen

Leader
The second question is: When shall we set off?
While this is being said, the piper moves towards the question mark 'When?' and calls her/him to join the line, moves around the church and then returns to the front.
When shall we set off? Listen to this.

12

Reader *(From off centre)*
    Acts 1.6-8

Prayer *(Led by 'When?')*
 Lord, forgive us for trying to organize your diary for you.
 Help us to trust your timetable for each of our lives.
 Then may we know that all times are right by you,
 for you are present in every breath, every hope, every step.
                    Amen

Leader
The third question is: Whose is the recommendation?
*While this is being said, the piper moves towards the question mark
'Whose?' and calls him/her to join the line, moves around the church, and
then returns to the front.*
Whose is the recommendation? Listen to this.

Reader *(From off centre)*
    John 10.14-16

Prayer *(Led by 'Whose?')*
 Jesus, shepherd and friend
 you yourself have trodden every path we are likely to tread;
 you know what it means to be hungry, to suffer, to hurt;
 you know what it means to laugh, to joke, to play;
 you not only tell us, you show us that this is the way to life, rich,
 full, and overflowing.
 Accept our prayer of praise and joy.   Amen

Leader
The fourth question is; Who is going with us?
*While this is being said, the piper moves towards the question mark 'Who?'
and calls her/him to join the line, moves around the church and returns to
the front*
Who is going with us? Listen to this.

Reader *(From off centre)*
    Matthew 5.3-11

Prayer   *(Led by 'Who?')*
So these are our strange companions, Lord,
the poor in spirit, the grief-stricken and downtrodden,
the merciful and peace-creators;
help us to look for them, to greet them and encourage them,
to share their joys and sorrows,
to be enriched by their lives.
Then we will be blessed indeed.   Amen

Hymn   'Jesus calls us!'
              or 'Living God, your joyful Spirit'

Leader
The fifth question is: What's on the programme?
*While this is being said, the piper moves towards the question mark 'What?'
and calls him/her to join the line, moves around the church, then returns to
the front.*
What's on the programme? Listen to this:

Reader   *(From off centre)*
              Luke 4.18-19

Prayer   *(Led by 'What?')*
Loving God,
you ask us to share with you in changing the world.
Give us the understanding and courage to stand up for justice;
give us the patience to work for peace;
give us the sensitivity to come alongside those who are in need,
as you have done in Jesus Christ.   Amen

Leader
The sixth question is: 'How much will it cost?'
*While this is being said, the piper moves towards the question mark 'How
much?' and calls her/him to join the line, moves around the church, then
returns to the front.*
How much will it cost? Listen to this:

Reader   *(From off centre)*
              Luke 9.23-24

14

Prayer   *(Led by 'How much?')*
Lord, this is where we think it hurts.
Help us to realize that when we follow you
we do not give things up, we take on more:
more joys, more sorrows, more forgiveness, more humour,
more interest in others, more life.
Thank you for paying the cost so we can live.   Amen

Leader
But there is one last, seventh, question: 'Why are we going?'
While this is being said the piper moves towards the question mark 'Why?'
and calls him/her to join the line, moves around the church, then returns to
the front.
Why are we going? Listen to this:

Reader   *(From off centre)*
                    1 Peter 2.9-10

Prayer   *(Led by 'Why?')*
Shine upon us, living God,
for you have called us from despair to hope, from death to life.
You have given us our lives
so that we can sing your praises;
you have called us out of darkness into your marvellous light.
Now we hear you saying to each of us:
'Come alive with my word of power.
Follow me into my glorious future.'
We offer ourselves to you and ask you to care for us each day,
through Jesus Christ our Lord.   Amen

Hymn   'One more step along the world I go'
During this hymn the Pied Piper moves through the congregation and out of
the sanctuary door (or other nearby exit) followed by the line of followers
including the question marks.

Benediction

15

MANY TIMES FORGIVEN

Introduction

Discipleship is not a journey for perfect people. The call to 'follow me' comes to individuals whose lives are unsettled and not yet fulfilled. Jesus calls those who have made mistakes, who are not totally reliable or who have problems with relationships. In short, the call comes to ordinary people, of all ages and backgrounds. There are no qualifications, exams, or tests. All that is needed is a grateful response and an awareness that the journey is worth making. Disciples are 'many times forgiven'. This service is most suitable for the beginning of Lent but can be adapted for other occasions. It provides a good opportunity in which to share bread and wine in family communion.

Preparation

Rehearse the different scenes choosing the participants carefully, and varying the age groups. Set up microphones where these are necessary. The Hosea scene needs a table, chair, writing material, waste-paper basket, and some acting ability by the person chosen.

The Jonah scene needs setting up in the style of a chat show. Produce cue cards to show the congregation when 'Applause' is needed, and prepare a group of younger people to respond with cheers, applause and screams. Provide a table, glasses of water etc. The part of the chat show host needs to be slightly over-played.

The Prodigal Son could be a child, dressed unkemptly.

The Lakeside scene needs a 'pretend' fire. The characters are nervous and uncertain, but must speak clearly.

Invite a family or other group in the church to prepare the forgiveness prayers used towards the end of the worship. They should use current newspapers to discover situations where forgiveness and reconciliation are present or needed.

ORDER OF SERVICE

Call to worship

Joel 2.12-14

Hymn   'Great is Thy faithfulness'
or 'O Lord, all the world belongs to you'

Prayer

God of every new day,
        every new beginning,
        every new moment,
we come to you
because you are eternally patient and forgiving.

Many, many times, we have hurt you and one another;
many, many times you have opened your arms to us,
accepting us and continuing to love us.

We offer you our praise today and every day.
Your patience amazes us; your love humbles us.
        Accept us yet again, as we seek to follow you.
        Through the life of Jesus your Son,
                remind us of how we too can forgive,
                how we too can live by love,
                how we too can help the world to live,
through Jesus' name we pray.

Amen

Hymn   'Jesus, Lover of my soul.' *(verses 3 & 4 only*
i.e. 'Thou, O Christ, art all I want' and
'Plenteous grace with thee is found')
or 'Amazing grace'

Leader

At the beginning of Lent we are reminded that we ourselves are wounded and torn. As individuals we often let down ourselves and our friends by what we say and do. As communities we fail to build a world of justice and peace. Again and again, we have to say sorry to God for the messes we get into and turn towards him for help in getting things right once more. The story of God's people is one of returning to God again and again. Look at four examples of this in the Bible: Hosea, Jonah, the Prodigal Son and Simon Peter.

Example 1: HOSEA

Focus on a table at which Hosea is writing a letter to his wife who has left him. He is in an agitated state. He struggles to find the words and often has to tear up the paper and start again.

HOSEA
Dear Gomer,
I don't know what to say. . . . where are you this time? . . . whether this letter will reach you, God knows. . . my heart feels . . . like a lead weight . . . one minute I am beside myself with anger, in grief, . . . the next I long for you to be back here with me, talking to me, eating at this table, in our home. Why, . . . why did you go yet again? Did you want more excitement, more money? I don't know what you see in those weird Canaanite practices . what about all those years we've shared? Please . . . if you read these words . . . please come back. . . leave the bright lights . . . I am sure it was not your fault entirely . . . others must have influenced you . . . you didn't understand . . . just remember . . . remember how it used to be with us . . . the good times we've had . . . how close we used to be . . .

Leader
Some of our Bible books have come out of the most painful and difficult of circumstances. The prophet Hosea was going through a not unusual but very sad experience: his wife Gomer had been consistently unfaithful to him. What hurt him more than ever, however, was that she had followed the attractions of Canaanite religion. All this made Hosea think hard about the sort of God he worshipped. He realized that God must feel exactly the same about his people as he felt about Gomer. They had persisted in running after all sorts of other gods and had been unfaithful again and again. They had not listened. They had not obeyed. They had forgotten who had loved them from the beginning. Listen to these words. They are not a lot different in feeling from the earlier ones we have just heard concerning his own marriage.

Reading Hosea 14.1-2; 4-7

Prayer
Gracious God, please forgive us yet again,
for our failure to worship you alone,
and to love you above the many other attractions around us.
We are sorry that we hurt you again and again through our
forgetfulness and apathy,
and yet we know that we can never be truly happy until we are
in harmony with your purposes for us.
Help us always to be thankful
for all your kindness and goodness
which you have showered upon us all our lives.
We ask this through Jesus Christ our Lord.   Amen

Hymn   'The love of God is broad like beach and meadow'
or 'Great God of wonders'

Example 2: JONAH

This second scene is a television interview with Jonah

HOST   Welcome to another edition of Wobegan *(caricature
                a current chat show host)* I'm your host and tonight I
                have a special guest. He has hit the headlines in all
                the tabloids recently following revelations that he
                has been swallowed, yes swallowed, by a large sea
                creature. The *Guardian* and *Independent,* however,
                avoided this sensational gossip and focussed
                instead on his experiences in Nineveh which
                turned out to be no less amazing. Please give a
                warm, dry, welcome to . . . Jonah!

show cue-card to congregation   (Applause, screams etc.)

HOST   Welcome, Jonah!
JONAH   Hi, I'm delighted to be here.
HOST   I bet you are. You've had a whale of a time. Your
                new book is compulsive reading!
JONAH   Thanks! You're right, I've had quite a time. It's a
                miracle I'm here really.

HOST	Tell us what was most important about your recent package holiday!
JONAH	Well, it's not the whale bit, I assure you. To tell you the truth, I'm quite ashamed. I've been taught the biggest lesson of my life.
HOST	What was that?
JONAH	Let me go back to the beginning. I didn't want to go to Nineveh. I'll admit that. That's why I got a one way ticket to the Costa del Tarshish. I knew at the time that it was wrong, but I did it . . . I ran off.
HOST	What was so awful about Nineveh? It's not a bad old city!
JONAH	It's an enormous city! And it is famous for its corruption. God wanted me to go there and tell them they would be destroyed unless they changed their ways.
HOST	Well, you went didn't you? Second time around you went!
JONAH	Of course I did. I gave them what for. And then it happened. . .
HOST	You mean the city was wiped out.
JONAH	You must be joking. I was astounded. All of them, from the king down, went and repented. They actually changed their life-style.
HOST	So what did you do?
JONAH	It's not me, it's God. I was still for wiping them off the face of the earth. After all, they're all foreigners, aren't they? But God had different ideas.
HOST	Like what?
JONAH	Like, forgiving them, that's what. I tell you, I was sick as a parrot. I went off into the desert and sulked like a child whose favourite toy had been taken away.
HOST	So is that why you were ashamed?
JONAH	I have learnt my lesson, and it was pretty earth-shattering. It seems that the people of these foreign nations are just as precious to God as we are. Imagine that! I'd always thought we were God's favourites.
HOST	Jonah, our time's up. And we've not talked about whales!

Show cue card for applause.

20

Leader
Jonah is a Hebrew story, a parable of forgiveness. Written at a time when foreigners were looked down upon by the Jews, it opens people's eyes to God's universal love. The name Jonah, son of Amittai, means 'Dove, son of Truth'. Jonah reminds every nation, every individual, that God has no special favourites. All are equally favoured, for God loves and forgives all who at any time follow his way.

Prayer
Lord,
many times we are judgemental of others.
We imagine that we are
    the only people you know,
    the only people you forgive,
    the only people you have time for.
Forgive us for our prejudice and jealousy.
Remind us that we don't deserve your care and patience.
Then, help us to forgive others,
and rejoice in their part in your Kingdom.   Amen

Prayer Responses   'Lord, to whom shall we go?' *and/or*
                       'Nothing in all creation' *and/or*
                       other songs/chorus' telling of God's forgiveness.

Example 3:   THE PRODIGAL SON

During the singing of the responses a dishevelled young man enters and moves towards the front. He is met and embraced by his parents.

Reading   Luke 15.21-24

Leader
Jesus told us a story which was both beautiful and controversial. It concerned a devoted father who had two sons. One took his inheritance and wasted it in another country. The father waited and waited, longing for his son to return. When he finally came home, the father ran down the street and welcomed him with open arms, then threw a big party. This story was told because there were lots of religious people who criticized Jesus for welcoming those who were outcast and on the edge of society. Jesus said the good news was

21

meant especially for those who felt they were out of range of God's love and forgiveness. He reminded them that they were many times forgiven, and so many times thankful.

Hymn   'Praise to the Holiest in the height' *(verses 1,2 & 7)*

Example 4:	**SIMON PETER**

In this scene some of the disciples are discussing the way they had reacted to Jesus' last week. They are seated around a fire by the lakeside.

JOHN	What day is it? I've lost all track of time these last few days.
JAMES	It's Tuesday. What a week!
JOHN	You look fed up.
JAMES	Well, I'm not exactly jumping for joy. Who could be after what we've been through. If you want the truth. I'm absolutely ashamed of myself.
JOHN	I know just what you mean. We all said we would follow Jesus to the end... you know... loyal supporters and all that. But who would have believed it would end like that!
JAMES	I don't know about you but I was scared to death on Friday... thought we'd all get crucified.
JOHN	It's simple. We freaked out. We were cowards. Even Peter...
PETER	*(Entering)* What's this you're saying?
JAMES	James was saying we all got scared.
PETER	I guess he's right. I was the one who was going to protect him and what did I do? I told them I wasn't even a disciple! I denied him three times! Me, Rocky! I don't know how I can look him in the eye again.
JOHN	We're all the same. The way he looked at you in the courtyard was the way he must have felt about us all.
JAMES	Seems years ago since we first met him doesn't it?
PETER	This lake brings it all back. 'Follow me, and I'll help you catch people.' Remember it? Fishing for people instead of fish! It sounded crazy.

| JOHN | But we followed. And we've certainly run into plenty of people! I'd never realized there was so much human need, so much to do. |
| PETER | Well, I'm hungry. Time we caught some fish. Anyone coming? |

Leader

So they went fishing, and they caught nothing. That is, until a stranger on the shore told them where the fish were shoaling. They did not recognize the stranger for some time. It was Jesus. When they shared breakfast they knew it was him all right.

Reading John 21.15-17

Leader

The ministering to people was to continue. Peter was being called as a disciple all over again. The work was going on. Peter the strong one, Peter the weak one, Peter the confident one, Peter the one who denied Jesus three times, that same mixed up lovable Peter was called all over again. Many times forgiven, he would now be a vital part of the kingdom.

Prayers

Use the series of short prayers prepared beforehand by children and adults on the theme of forgiveness. As the prayers come to an end Hosea, Jonah, the Prodigal Son and Simon Peter move among the congregation shaking hands. The leader should identify the action as a sign of reconciliation. Bread and wine may be shared as signs of the new covenant of forgiveness into which we all enter.

Hymn   'The right hand of God is writing in our land'

Benediction

LIVING WATER

Introduction

Water is one of the most common commodities, but it is very precious. Deprived of water, human beings, animals and the earth soon become frail and lifeless. Water has therefore become a symbol of life, renewal, and health.

This service explores the symbol of water with particular reference to certain key biblical passages. It may be particularly suitable for occasions of baptism and/or confirmation, or when the whole congregation renews its commitment to discipleship. With adaptation this service can also be used for a service of healing or one in which people are commissioned for particular tasks and ministries. If it is linked with Jesus' baptism, the service would be appropriate for Epiphany; equally, if associated with the anointing at Bethany or the foot-washing in the upper room, it could be used in Holy Week.

Preparation

Try to enhance the setting for worship by inviting families and individuals to create miniature 'water gardens' on the window-sills around the sanctuary.

Choose a person (if the church has a central isle), or two (if there are side aisles), to be 'water seller/s' at the beginning. Ideally, use a trolley and different kinds of cups, mugs and containers. Alternatively plan a cinema-style waiter/waitress service with various people carrying trays with plastic cups of water. Only small amounts of water need be provided in the cups.

Provide bowls of water and leafy sprigs for sprinkling the congregation. People will need to be assigned to carry the bowls and others to wave the leafy sprigs.

'Storm music' and 'peace music' will be needed. If the pianist or organist cannot provide this, find suitable pieces of recorded music (suggestions are made in the Order of Service).

Three readers (Voices 1, 2 and 3 are required).

ORDER OF SERVICE

The 'water-seller(s)' (see preparation) enters from the back of the sanctuary, or other entrance nearby. A drink of water is offered to as many members of the congregation as possible. Others follow with large bowls of water which are placed conspicuously at the front of the church. Some are placed on the communion table. While this is happening a group quietly sings the following verse: (possible tunes include Kingsfold and Vox Dilecti).

I heard the voice of Jesus say,
'Behold I freely give
The living water; thirsty one,
Stoop down, and drink and live.'
I came to Jesus, and I drank
Of that life-giving stream;
My thirst was quenched, my soul revived,
And now I live in Him.

Horatius Bonar

As the water distributor(s) reaches the front, a reader slowly reads:

Reading   Isaiah 55.1-3, 6-7

Leader
'Come to the waters!' says the prophet. That is God's invitation. In other words: come and accept what I am offering to you free of charge. Come and share my life. You'll find there's plenty of it. It's rich; more like wine than water! It doesn't depend on your income or your goodness or your level of commitment. It is freely offered. All you have to do is accept it as a gift.

Prayer
Where the words can be duplicated or an overhead projector used then the whole congregation should speak the prayer.

Living God
we depend on you
for the breath in our bodies
and the love in our hearts;
we rely on you for the fruitfulness of the ground
and the energy in the earth.

You have given us everything we need
for a full and rich life together.
Today in worship we thank you once more,
and gladly accept the gifts you bring to us.
Accept this prayer
in the name of Jesus Christ our Lord.   Amen

Hymn   'The King of love my Shepherd is'
            or 'For the beauty of the earth'
Leader
For Christians, all the goodness and gifts that God offers to the world
are brought into focus in one special person, Jesus Christ. If we need
reminding of all we owe to God we need look no further. Jesus is
God's unique and precious gift. Jesus was baptized as a sign that he
was adopted by God for a special purpose. It was a sign of God's
commitment to all his people.

PROMISE

Reading   Isaiah 43.1-4

Leader
The story of God's people is the account of God's commitment to his
people and his world. He will never leave his people on their own.
They are never orphans. They are eternally loved. When they pass
through dark and dangerous times, God does not abandon them. He
accompanies them, He is alongside them. Jesus is a living sign of that
promise. Jesus shares his disciples questions and fears. He deals with
their anger and frustration. He calms the storms of their
disappointment. He offers peace in time of danger.

Hymn   'Do not be afraid, for I have redeemed you'
            or 'How firm a foundation, ye saints of the Lord'

RESOURCE

Reading   John 4.7-15
*The water distributor(s) may offer more water to the congregation at this
point.*

Leader

Not only does God promise to stay with his people, he also provides resources to sustain them. When the woman of Samaria came to the well to draw water, she met a person who offered a different kind of water. Jesus had come into the world offering life in all its fullness. It was not available to one race only, or to men only. It was offered to Samaritans as well as Jews, even though the two peoples had been enemies for centuries. It was offered to women as well as men, although women had been treated as inferior in both Israel and Samaria.

Prayer of Confession

Where the words can be duplicated or an overhead projector used then the whole congregation should speak the prayer.

    Lord, our lives are dried up,
    they lack freshness and vigour;
    they respond so slowly to human need;
    they are not motivated to go extra miles in service.
    We are thirsty for the life-giving water;
    we long to draw from the reservoirs of your love,
    so that we are refreshed and invigorated.
    Fill us with new life and joy,
    restore within us the wonder of faith
    and the courage of hope.
    We ask this in Jesus' name.   Amen

Hymn   'Jesus, lover of my soul'

Suggest that this be sung as an assurance of forgiveness and draw particular attention to verse four; 'plenteous grace with thee is found'.

Leader

    Living water is offered to us all.
        This is the invitation.
    Living water is a sign that God will not abandon us.
        This is the promise.
    Living water is available all the time to all disciples of Jesus.
        This is the resource.
    Let us now sing of these three discoveries.

Hymn   'I heard the voice of Jesus say'

During this hymn more bowls of water may be brought to the front of the church.

Leader
Now let's dream a bit. What kind of world does God want? What sort of villages, towns and cities? What kind of families, friendships, communities? What kind of government, industry, schools? If Jesus provides us with Living Water, and is a sign of new life for each of us, then how can this transform the places where we live, work and play?

VISION

During the following section play 'storm music' in the background. Some pianists/organists will be able to improvise. Alternatively, the storm section of Beethoven's 'Pastoral Symphony' or the 'Sea Interlude' from the opera 'Peter Grimes' by Benjamin Britten can be used. The voices should be 'voices off' but make sure that they can be heard above the music.

Leader
At the beginning of the Bible water is a danger, a threat of fearful danger. It is a sign of God's judgement:

VOICE 1   I am going to bring a flood of waters on the earth, to destroy from under heaven all flesh in which is the breath of life; everything that is on the earth shall die.

Genesis 6.17 (NRSV)

During the following section play calm and peaceful music. If recorded music is needed use the 'Sunday morning 'Sea Interlude' by Benjamin Britten or some gentle piano music.

Leader
By the end of the Bible, water is a healing stream, the river of the water of life.

VOICE 2   Then the angel showed me the river of the water of life, bright as crystal, flowing from the throne of God and of the Lamb through the middle of the street of the city.

VOICE 3   On either side of the river is the tree of life with its twelve kinds of fruit, producing its fruit each month; and the leaves of the tree are for the healing of the nations.

Revelation 22.1-2 (NRSV)

Hymn   'For the healing of the nations'
During this hymn people come in carrying leafy sprigs

Prayers for the world
Use short prayers of intercession for people and places where healing is needed, and for those who share in the task of caring. Make these topical.

TASK

Leader
The vision will remain only a dream unless we work to realize it. We share in Christ's baptism and are adopted by God to share in his work. The task is twofold:

VOICE 1   Go therefore and make disciples of all nations, baptizing them in the name of the Father and of the Son and of the Holy Spirit, teaching them to observe all that I have commanded you; and remember, I am with you always, to the end of the age.
Matthew 28.19-20 (NRSV)

VOICE 2   If I, your Lord and Teacher, have washed your feet, you also ought to wash one another's feet. For I have set you an example, that you also should do as I have done to you.
John 13.14-15 (NRSV)

Leader
These are the two tasks given to us. First, 'Baptize all nations'. That means more than offering the sacrament of baptism; it means sharing the good news and helping others to become friends of Jesus. Secondly, 'Wash one another's feet'. That means serving each other, going the extra mile of listening, caring, forgiving, making peace, and loving your neighbours.
Where possible include the sacrament of baptism at this point, or if the service is being held in Holy Week there could be a symbolic foot-washing.

Hymn   'Glorious things of thee are spoken'
          or 'Jesu, Jesu, fill us with your love'
During this hymn the people with leafy sprigs move among the congregation waving the sprigs which have been dipped in the bowls of water at the front of the church.

Prayer of Commitment
Where the words can be duplicated or an overhead projector used then the whole congregation should speak the prayer.
Jesus,
friend of the world,
source of living water for all peoples,
accept our promise to follow you
each step of our lives
as we tell others of your amazing love
and serve one another in your name.   Amen

Benediction

CITY OF PALMS

Introduction

This is a service of celebration focussing on Jerusalem as the goal of Jesus' journey. The differing hopes of all those participating in Palm Sunday are explored as a basis for asking such questions as: 'What are our expectations of this day? What are our hopes for our world? Who are we following to achieve these hopes?'

Preparation

Scripts need to be given ahead of time to the main characters in the celebration. Some of the participants will benefit from being dressed up, or by wearing appropriate head-dresses or masks (e.g. donkey, palm trees, doves). They should all be readily identifiable e.g. by wearing a sash bearing their name. The setting for the interviews would be improved by having signs such as 'The West Gate' (for interviews 1 & 2); 'The Castle' (interview 3); 'The Palace' (interview 4); 'The Temple' (interviews 5 & 6). The Interviewer, equipped with a microphone has a key role. Choose someone with a strong voice and the ability to keep a conversation flowing. S/he should move to different locations for each interview, the appropriate sign being held up at that place.

ORDER OF SERVICE

Call to worship *Read from the back of the congregation*
Zechariah 9.9-12

Hymn 'Hail to the Lord's anointed'
or 'All glory, laud and honour'

In the final verse of the hymn the people taking part in the 'Introduction of the theme' move to their places in the groupings suggested for the interviews.

Prayer

> Gracious God
> we have many confused hopes
> many unfulfilled dreams.
> As we greet Jesus on another Palm Sunday,
> Help us to look beyond ourselves
> to see your hopes and dreams for the world
> as well as our own.
> As we sing 'Hosanna' once more,
> may our songs be a sign of commitment
> to the way of sacrifice,
> the path of peace-making
> and the road to dedicated service.
> Through Jesus Christ our Lord.   Amen

Leader (*Introduction of the theme*)

Everybody involved in the Palm Sunday drama had their hopes for that festival season. As the drama proceeds you can almost hear them saying, 'I wish . . . I wish . . . I wish . . .'

CHILDREN	I wish the procession would start. Let's get more palm branches to wave!
PALM TREES	I wish they'd stop stealing our branches. Hear, hear! You'd think someone would tell them about conservation!
DONKEY	I'm bored! I wish I were a horse!
PRIESTS	I wish this troublemaker Jesus would stay away.
PILATE	I wish we didn't have to have these religious festivals. There's always trouble!
TWO FRIENDS OF JESUS	I wish we'd stayed in Galilee! I wish I knew what Jesus is up to!
MARTHA	He's coming! Got to get the house cleaned - and he's staying here on Wednesday! I'll never get everything done, - especially at Passover time!
TWO ROMAN SOLDIERS	I hear there's a so called Messiah on a donkey. Now there's a novel way to take the city by storm!
JUDAS	Now's my chance! The priests would love to be rid of him!
MARY	Something dreadful is going to happen. I'm scared.
TWO DOVES	Tweet! Is it you or me for the sacrifice this year? Tweet! Tweet! If you ask me it's time to fly!

If it is difficult to find enough people for the parts, the parts of Mary Magdalene, one soldier, one dove and Pilate can be omitted. Alternatively, one person could play the part of the donkey, the doves, a palm tree and show the change of character by deliberately changing a head-dress to indicate the change.

Jesus enters (or voice off)

JESUS   O Jerusalem, if only you knew what leads to peace. But you don't even recognize your deliverer when he comes! I weep because I love you and I fear for your future.

Leader

I wish, I wish, I wish . . . We all wish for someone, something to change this sad and weary world into a place of beauty, peace and justice

Hymn   'O come, O come Immanuel'
              or 'Make way, make way'

Interviews

Using a roving radio style, interview the characters who have expressed their wishes in the drama. Explore their hopes and fears for Palm Sunday and Holy Week. Do this by drawing the characters together in groups, each interview followed by a short prayer and hymn/song. The following scripts are only intended as guidance. The interviewer must take the lead and initiate the conversation.

INTERVIEW 1	Two palm trees and two children

INTERVIEWER   There seems to be something exciting going on here. What's happening?

CHILD 1   Where have you been all morning?

CHILD 2   You must be the only person in town who hasn't heard. It's happening at last. Honest! Everybody says so.

INTERVIEWER   OK, OK . . . so what's going on?

PALM 1   Don't get all worked up. It's just another demonstration.

PALM 2   Some silly prophet the people have gone crackers about.

PALM 1   It means we're going to get shorn again!

PALM 2   Who'd be a palm tree!

33

CHILD 1	But it is exciting! This time it will be different.
CHILD 2	This man's different. He's going to free us all!
CHILD 1	They say he can make the blind see and the lame walk!
PALM 1	And stick palm leaves back onto their branches?
PALM 2	He'll be king for the day, like all the others!
INTERVIEWER	So he's a king?
CHILD 2	He's not on his high horse. He's gentle and friendly.
CHILD 1	We've heard he's riding on a donkey. I don't see why the whole world doesn't like him.
CHILD 1 & 2	Hosanna! Hosanna!

Prayer

Loving God, you have never waited for us to come to you.
Instead, you have come to us:
born in busy Bethlehem,
reaching out to people in Galilee;
healing, serving, forgiving, welcoming;
always trying to help us to live together in peace.
Now accept our welcome, our greeting, our Hosannas.
Give us the enthusiasm of children
and the gratitude of those who know that they need you as
Saviour and Lord. Amen

Hymn 'We have a king who rides on a donkey' *(verses of)*
or 'Children of Jerusalem'

INTERVIEW 2	Martha, Mary Magdalene (MARY M), and two friends of Jesus

INTERVIEWER	I've heard you are close friends of this Jesus king?
FRIEND 1	That's right, I'm Levi, I've been with him from the start.
FRIEND 2	I'm Philip, another of his disciples.
INTERVIEWER	So why's he making this protest, or whatever it is?
FRIEND 1	Don't get the wrong idea. He's not a showman. He's trying to get people to remember what Zechariah prophesied years ago.
INTERVIEWER	What was that?
MARY M	Let me tell you. I'm Mary Magdalene. First, this man's a kind generous, forgiving, genuine person.

34

	Zechariah said a king would come who was gentle and peace-loving.
MARTHA	He stayed at our house the last couple of nights. I was too busy to hear much of what he was saying, but I'll tell you this, he knows that the authorities have got it in for him.
INTERVIEWER	You mean he's in danger?
FRIEND 1	Most people don't want peace. They want a war and a warrior - anyone who will get rid of the Romans.
FRIEND 2	We're afraid for him. He seems determined to show Jerusalem a different way to freedom and permanent peace.
MARY M	I wonder if we'll still say we're his friends by the end of the week?

Prayer

Forgive us, patient God,
for our feeble commitment to your way.
We follow when the crowds are excited and happy,
but we hide when there's danger and fear.
Accept our thanks for Jesus' single-minded vision and help us
not to be afraid to say we are his friends when people are violent
and peace and love are crucified,
through Jesus Christ our Lord.   Amen

Hymn   'My song is love unknown' *(use selected verses)*

INTERVIEW 3	Pilate and the Roman Soldiers

INTERVIEWER	I'm very grateful to you for allowing me this audience. This must be a very disturbing time for you.
PILATE	No more disturbing than most. It's Passover, of course. Always trouble at the Passover. The Jews get very excited.
INTERVIEWER	I'd like to know your opinion concerning the demonstration in the city today.
PILATE	I expect you mean the one involving that Jesus of Nazareth fellow. Nothing to write home about. Minor parade. Bit ridiculous actually. We've kept our eyes on it.

INTERVIEWER	Sounds like this prophet was claiming to be a king.
PILATE	King? You must be joking. On a donkey? Hardly an armed insurrection. Caesar will be shaking! I can see the headlines in the *Roman Chronicle,* 'Caesar toppled by one man and a donkey!'
INTERVIEWER	If this develops into something bigger, how will you handle it?
PILATE	My job is to keep the peace. Riots can break out over nothing. Even donkeys. So I will make sure the city stays calm.
INTERVIEWER	Can I have a word with one or two of your soldiers on the way out?
PILATE	Of course, be my guest, but don't hang around.
INTERVIEWER	*(turning to two soldiers)* Have you anything to say about the mood of the city right now?
SOLDIER 1	Pretty normal, if you ask me.
SOLDIER 2	Bit of trouble near one of the gates this morning. Nothing much to worry about.
SOLDIER 1	I hate festival time. Unpredictable.
SOLDIER 2	There's bound to be trouble while we hold people like Barabbas!
SOLDIER 1	We've said enough. Move along now . . . please!
INTERVIEWER	OK, OK, I'm going.

Prayer

God of history, of all nations and centuries,
as the years roll by,
we see events come and go,
empires rise and fall,
and we feel powerless to change what goes on.
Remind us today
how Jesus' strange and quiet way
can transform the lives of individuals and nations.
Forgive us for washing our hands of true justice
because we fail to see your hand on history.
Give us courage to see in Jesus
the path to true power and glory.
In his name we ask it.   Amen

Hymn   'It is a thing most wonderful'

36

INTERVIEW 4	Priests, Judas

INTERVIEWER   A quick word, your highnesses, please.
PRIEST 1   What do you want?
PRIEST 2   We're very busy!
PRIEST 1   Didn't you realize it's Passover week!
PRIEST 2   We're off to the Temple now.
INTERVIEWER   I've only one question.
PRIEST 1   And what's that?
INTERVIEWER   Have you any comment on the Jesus of Nazareth episode?
PRIEST 2   He's a blasphemer.
INTERVIEWER   What do you mean?
PRIEST 1   He breaks the law! He's a menace.
INTERVIEWER   But the people love him!
PRIEST 2   Rubbish! He can't free them. He's a fool!
PRIEST 1   Out of our way!
INTERVIEWER   OK, OK. By the way, didn't I just see one of Jesus' disciples hanging around a minute ago?
PRIEST 2   Didn't you hear? Out of our way.
INTERVIEWER   *(Turning to Judas)* Aren't you one of Jesus' friends?
JUDAS   Who, Me?
INTERVIEWER   Yes, you! What are you doing round here?
JUDAS   What do you mean?
INTERVIEWER   Why have you been talking to the priests?
JUDAS   You're mistaken, mate. *(He rushes away)*

Prayer

God of those who think they are holy
and those who know they are not.
Forgive us if we have obstructed your purposes.
When we disown you and discredit your name,
when we follow our own selfish ends,
please forgive us and help us to change.
We are ashamed of your church when,
lost in power-seeking and hypocrisy,
it has failed you, denied you, and broken your heart.
Please accept our confession and sorrow.
Our prayer we bring in Jesus' name.

Amen

37

Hymn   'Kyrie Eleison' *(Iona community)*
or other hymn expressing forgiveness

INTERVIEW 5	The Two doves and the donkey

INTERVIEWER	Just a minute, before you fly off. Can I have a word with you?
DOVE 1	Tweet! Tweet!
DOVE 2	Tweet! Tweet!
INTERVIEWER	This is a tough time of the year for you, isn't it?
DOVE 1	You mean it's sacrifice time, and all that? Danger time?
INTERVIEWER	That's right.
DOVE 2	We may be lucky and get away.
INTERVIEWER	Did you see what happened this morning?
DOVE 1	If you're talking about the demonstration, yes, I was in the nearby palm tree.
DOVE 2	Me too.
INTERVIEWER	What did you make of it?
DOVE 1	I liked the fellow. Quiet. I don't think it was a rip off like a lot of things at Passover time.
DOVE 2	I agree. He's a dove not a hawk, I reckon.
DOVE 1	Why don't you have a word with the donkey over there?
DOVE 2	He was as near to the action as anyone!
INTERVIEWER	Thanks! *(Turning to the donkey)* Have you got a moment?
DONKEY	Sure, but I'm all in!
INTERVIEWER	What did you make of your passenger?
DONKEY	Marvellous! Strong, gentle, just ideal. Why he chose me I'll never know!
INTERVIEWER	Seems to have a habit of doing the unexpected.
DONKEY	He seems to be very popular. But I noticed the priests and scribes chuntering. I think they're cooking something nasty.
INTERVIEWER	You think he's in danger?
DONKEY	I do. I think they're out to get him. Such a good man too.

38

Prayer

> God of surprises,
> You have often chosen the humble and meek
> in order to overthrow the proud and self-centred.
> We pray for all who in their humble and quiet way
> are your servants in the world,
> carrying the pain of others,
> sharing human suffering and grief,
> lifting human burdens.
> Be with all your faithful people
> who, in the heat of the day,
> are true followers of Jesus,
> your Son and our Lord.   Amen

Hymn   'The glory of our king was seen'
           or 'Trotting, trotting'

INTERVIEW 6	Jesus

INTERVIEWER	Jesus, Jesus, please, can I just have a quick word?
JESUS	Of course, it's no trouble.
INTERVIEWER	Why did you do it?
JESUS	You mean, enter the city in this way?
INTERVIEWER	Yes.
JESUS	It was just a sign. A sign of the kingdom of God. A sign that children and grown-ups can look back on and understand. My kingdom is not of this world. I am not an earthly king like Caesar.
INTERVIEWER	So what's next?
JESUS	Well, you'll have to wait and see. Anything can happen. I'm not absolutely sure myself. But I assure you everything I do will be so that the world can be changed into a different place. God loves this city . . . and every city. If only people knew the way to peace!
INTERVIEWER	Thank you, Master . . . and . . . good luck! . . . I mean . . . God bless you!

Prayers
Invite the congregation to offer silent prayer, directing them as follows:
 pray for peace in the world *(mention topical places and events).*
 pray for a just future.
 pray for new insights in this coming Holy Week.

Hymn   'Lord Jesus Christ, you have come to us'

Benediction

ACKNOWLEDGEMENTS

Every effort has been made to trace copyright owners but if any rights have been inadvertently overlooked, the necessary correction will be made in subsequent editions. We apologise for any apparent negligence.

We are grateful to quote from the following version of the Bible:

NRSV   *New Revised Standard Version Bible* (© 1989 by Division of Christian Education of the National Council of Christ in the USA).

MORE RESOURCES FOR ALL AGE WORSHIP FROM NCEC

CELEBRATING SERIES

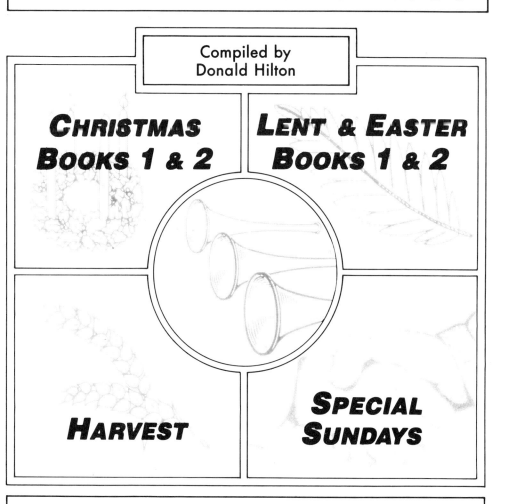

Compiled by
Donald Hilton

CHRISTMAS BOOKS 1 & 2

LENT & EASTER BOOKS 1 & 2

HARVEST

SPECIAL SUNDAYS

FESTIVAL SERVICES for the Church Year

Sold individually or in a set with a substantial saving

Available from all good Christian bookshops or, in case of difficulty, from NCEC direct.

Other Titles from RADIUS and NCEC

Who'll
be
Brother
Donkey?

by
Arthur Scholey

THE HILL
Sylvia Read
0-7197-0761-7

A modern mystery play in which the characters find themselves caught up in the experience of Easter. 30 mins.

Code No. PLA0761 (A)

CROSSTALK
Bob Irving
0-7197-0795-1

A collection of ten short plays based upon the parables which were, in their own time, sharp contemporary stories in an established tradition. In order to convey the same sense of immediacy these sketches are presented in a highly modern quick-firing style. No need for props or costumes, maximum cast of five. Each play lasts about 5 minutes.

Code No. PLA0795 (A)

SURPRISE SKETCHES
Ronald Rich
0-7197-0796-X

Five one-act plays with surprising endings. Ideal as a prompter for discussion or for use in worship, these plays examine some familiar human failings in a new stimulating style. Each play runs for about 10 minutes.

Code No. PLA0796 (A)

THE FLAME
Edmund Banyard
0-7197-0709-9

A novel approach to the idea of Pentecost, this play is a one act fantasy in the style of the Theatre of the Absurd. Four ordinary people are offered the 'Light of the World' by a messenger from the border between Time and Eternity. 25 mins.

Code No. FLA0709 (A)

> Performance times given are
> very approximate.

A FISTFUL OF FIVERS
Edmund Banyard
0-7197-0667-X

Twelve five-minute plays, each with a Christian message. Using the minimum of actors, scenery and props, these lively sketches will appeal to everyone who is young in the widest sense.

Code No. PLA0667 (A)

A FUNNY THING HAPPENED ON THE WAY TO JERICHO
Tom Long
0-7197-0722-6

The dress rehearsal for a presentation of the Good Samaritan turns out to be more than the leading player intended, as she is challenged by each of the roles she takes on in her search for the one she feels happy with. 30 mins.

Code No. FUN0722 (A) R

THE PRODIGAL DAUGHTER
William Fry
0-7197-0668-8

Using a neat twist, William Fry has turned one of the best-known parables into the tale of a present-day girl, updating the setting to portray some of the concerns of modern society. While it shows the seamier side of contemporary life, the message of this play is ultimately one of redemption and love. 30 mins.

Code No. PLA0668 (A)

NATIVITY LETTERS
Nick Warburton
0-7197-0724-2

Highlights the strains put on mother and daughter in the interdependence of a single parent family, which make them tend to disassociate themselves from other people. Help eventually presents itself through a committed teacher in the daughter's drama group. 40 mins.

Code No. NAT0724 (A)

WHO'LL BE BROTHER DONKEY?
Arthur Scholey
0-7197-0723-4

Three traditional Christmas tales are combined to produce this play where the animals use their Christmas Eve gift of speech to enact the crib scene in the hillside chapel. During the journey from their stable they outwit the wily Fox and Vixen in their malevolent schemes. The conclusion shows how the preparation of the crib scene is achieved against all odds through forgiveness of their fellow creatures and faith. 60 mins.

Code No. WHO0723 (A)